Mrs John Rolfe of Heacham

better known as

Pocahontas

by

John Haden and the Pupils of
Heacham Junior School, Norfolk

First published by Barny Books,
All rights reserved
Copyright © 2006 John Haden

2nd Edition 2014
Copyright © 2014 John Haden

No part of this publication may be reproduced or transmitted in any way or by any means, including electronic storage and retrieval, without prior permission of the publisher.

ISBN No: 978-1-906542-66-5

Publishers: Barny Books, 11 Millfield Crescent,
Caythorpe, Grantham
Lincolnshire
NG32 3HG UK

Tel: +44 (0)1400 273489

Copies of this book and the others in the ARIES series may be obtained from the Publisher or from:

ARIES Project
13 St Albans Close, Oakham
Rutland LE15 6EW
Tel: 01572 720428

Please enclose cheque payable to 'Julian Bower Associates' with your order and add £1.00 per copy to cover postage and packing.

Or on-line from Amazon.co.uk, via 'new: ARIES Project' as seller.

Contents

1. Foreword   4

2. Who was John Rolfe of Heacham?   6

3. Going to Virginia   16

4. Powhatan's daughter   31

5. Mr and Mrs John Rolfe   50

6. Going to England   66

7. Pocahontas' people   81

8. And is it true?   84

9. Sources and thanks   88

1. Foreword

Two English coastal communities share an interest in an exotic character from the early Seventeenth Century, the Virginian Indian Princess best known as Pocahontas. .

Gravesend on the Thames estuary was the place ships called at on their way from London to the distant corners of the world. It was also the place where Pocahontas died. She was buried in the graveyard of St George's Parish Church, where you will find her statue, and a brief mention of the Englishman she married.

Heacham in Norfolk was the birthplace of John Rolfe, the father of the Virginia tobacco industry and husband of Pocahontas. There is a picture of Pocahontas on the village sign and a memorial in the church but there is no tomb of John Rolfe. Even the Rolfe family home, Heacham Hall, is now burnt down.

The story of Pocahontas is for ever connected with another hero, Captain John Smith. She is said to have saved his life and so saved the Jamestown colony, which is probably true. The story of John Smith, Pocahontas and John Rolfe has inspired books, songs and pictures, and most recently films, but few of these tell the full true story.

This book has been written and illustrated with the help of pupils and teachers from Heacham Junior School, Norfolk. It was first published to commemorate the 400th anniversary of the founding of Jamestown, Virginia, the first permanent English-speaking settlement in America. This revised edition has been published to celebrate the 400th anniversary of the Christian conversion of Pocohontas and the Rolfe-Pocahontas wedding. We hope that you enjoy reading our account of what really happened in the lives of Mr and Mrs John Rolfe and will also enjoy reading the other titles in the American Roots in English Soil Series (ARIES) of books written with schools.

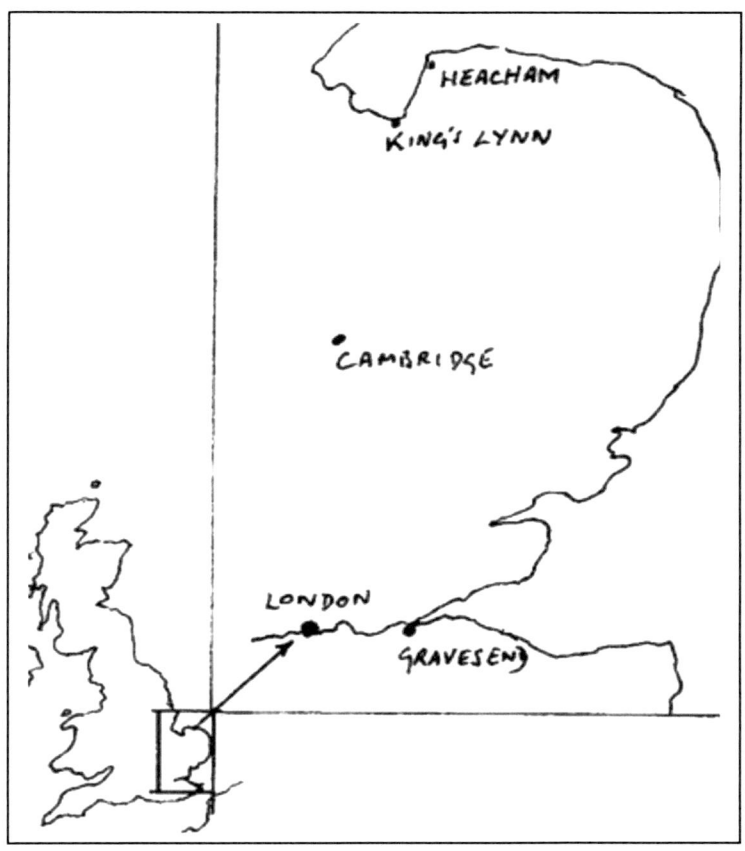

Sketch map of Eastern England showing Norfolk and King's Lynn in the County of Norfolk

2. Who was John Rolfe of Heacham?

This old photograph tell the story of a Norfolk family. They were rich enough to own a large house with well kept grounds in the village of Heacham, in the remote north-west corner of the County of Norfolk.

For hundreds of years right up to the early twentieth century, members of the Rolfe family lived at Heacham Hall. The Tudor building was replaced by a bigger house in Georgian times and that in turn was demolished and a new Hall built around the start of the last century shortly before the picture was taken. The Rolfes lived in comfort and style, with a team of servants to cook and clean, cut the grass and look after them. As the owners of the largest house in the village and much of the land around Heacham, they were respected members of the local community, enjoying English country life.

Today, there is no Hall building in Heacham because it was burnt down in the 1940s when the Armed Forces were using it during World War II. It was never rebuilt but the large park which surrounded the Hall is still there. The gates that lead into the park from the village green are just opposite the church.

Heacham Parish Church

The Heacham Rolfes were not as rich as the great Norfolk families, like the Cokes of Holkam Hall to the east, or as old as those who came with the Norman conquest and built their castles and priories at Castle Acre and Castle Rising to the south. They were typical of families who became rich in Tudor England after the great monasteries were closed and their lands redistributed to any who had the money to buy them.

The Rolfes brought their children to the Parish Church of St Mary the Virgin to be baptised in the old font which is still used today. They came too, to be married in the church and many were buried inside or in the graveyard which surrounds the old building. When the church-yard was full, one of the Rolfes gave an acre of land for more burials. 'Rolfe's Acre' is still there with a corner kept for members of the family. Some are also remembered with monuments in the church.

Over four hundred years ago in the fourth year of the reign of Queen Elizabeth I, Eustace Rolfe of Heacham Hall, brought his son, John, to be baptised at this font.

The Font in Heacham Parish

This John was the father of our John Rolfe of Heacham, so we can call him 'John Rolfe Senior'. There is a memorial plaque made of brass in the North Aisle of the Church, which has a Latin text including this tribute, '*he increased his family estate with the export and import of things which England either abounded with or wanted*'.

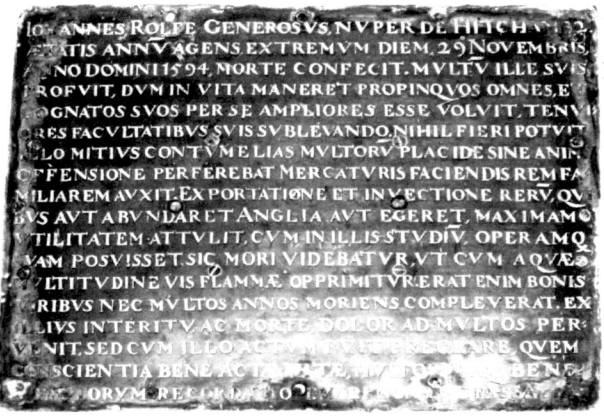

Memorial to John Rolfe's father in Heacham Parish Church

In other words, John Rolfe's father was a successful merchant in the nearby port of King's Lynn. He made money from selling wool and corn from the rich farmland of England to merchants in the cities of Northern Europe which had formed the Hanseatic League, an early form of European Common Market. English merchants like Rolfe imported wine, timber and other goods from these cities, to sell at a good profit in Elizabethan England. Rolfe used his wealth to buy more land around Heacham and when he had enough money and land, he acquired the status of gentleman with his own coat of arms and the right to put 'esquire' after his name.

There are examples of the Rolfe family arms in the panels displayed high on the walls of the nave of the church. On the north side, two of the panels belong to Rolfes and have their wheatsheaf, gold rings and eight-segmented square or 'gyronny'. On the opposite wall, the arms show the same symbols combined with the elements of their widows' family arms, such as the three running dogs in the central hatchment.

When John Rolfe Senior was twenty, he married Dorothy Mason, in the same church. Three years later in 1585, they brought their twin sons to be baptised. The eldest, Eustace, was named after his grandfather, and the second, John, after his father. Eustace died as a child but the younger twin, John, grew up at Heacham. There were three more children born to John and Dorothy: Henry, Edward and Dorothy. Henry and Edward come into this story but little is known about Dorothy.

There is no record of where John Rolfe went to school although the quality of his writing later in life shows that he must have had a good education. His family probably provided him with a tutor at home.

Tudor schools

It was very hard growing up in those times. Many poor people's children did not go to school at all. Some boys and girls were taught by the priest in parish schools, where they learned the alphabet and how to read and write. Girls did not go to school after they were seven.

Most of the towns, like Fakenham, had a grammar school, but poor boys could not afford to go. Only very rich children had their own teachers at home. Boys started at grammar school at the age of seven. The main subject was Latin and they were also taught some arithmetic and some Bible stories. There was no P.E. or science.

The school day lasted from about seven in the morning to four o'clock in the afternoon, the teachers were

very strict and they very often beat the boys with rods of birch twigs. I think this was very bad, even in 1600!
(by Rebecca)

When John was nine, his father died and his mother re-married. Her second husband was Dr Robert Redmayne, who became the Mayor of King's Lynn and the Chancellor of the Norwich Diocese. Dr Redmayne's fine monument is in the north aisle of Heacham Parish Church and Dorothy's simple grave slab in the floor below. She outlived him by twenty years and you can just make out the battered inscription

'in the 80th yeare of her age ...at the feet of her two husbands. ....beloved and lovely! In life and death, they were not divided.' (2 Samuel 1 v 23)

Like most of the Norfolk gentry of their day, the Rolfes were deeply religious in the Calvinist tradition.

When he was in his early twenties, John Rolfe himself married although there is no record of his wife's name or the date of the wedding. The young couple might have stayed in quiet obscurity in rural Norfolk if John had not heard of exciting opportunities offered by the Virginia Company of London. They were raising money and recruiting settlers to live in their tiny colony at Jamestown, Virginia, three thousand miles away across the Atlantic Ocean.

In 1607, the Virginia Company had sent three small ships with 104 men and boys to establish a settlement on the banks of the James River. Thanks to the leadership of one of the colonists, Captain John Smith, and to the friendship he established with the Algonquian speaking people of Virginia, the colony had survived.

John Rolfe's mother's grave slab in the floor of Heacham Church

Coat of Arms of Catherine, wife of Edmund Rolfe of Heacham who died in 1837

Heacham Parish Church – a lively centre of worship today

The Elizabethan part of the Guild Hall, King's Lynn, next to the original 1421 Hall

Jamestown in trouble

After John Smith left, sickness, famine and lack of leadership very nearly caused the Jamestown Colony to be abandoned. Men who had set out from England with high hopes of finding gold and a new way through to the riches of the spice islands of the Pacific Ocean had found neither. The settlement was still dependent on supplies of corn from the "Indians" and they were increasingly unwilling to feed the English.

According to the records kept by the Treasurer of the London Virginia Company, John Rolfe's brother Henry had invested £12 10s in the Company. It may be that John was also an investor, as there is a record of 'John Wroth' investing £87 10s. Wroth, Rolffe and Rolfe were all possible spellings of the family name at a time when people's spelling even of their own name was not fixed. Shakespeare certainly spelt his name many different ways! Either way, the brothers were clearly interested in the Virginia Company's plan to set up and develop a new English colony on the shores of North America. They wanted to be part of this new adventure.

In June 1609, the Company sent out notices to all the towns and cities of England inviting 'merchants and gentlemen' to join their new colony. John Rolfe may have read the notice on one of his frequent visits to the town of King's Lynn. Perhaps he took a copy back back to Heacham to discuss with his young wife. They decided that this new opportunity offered them a better future than staying in England. In any case even if they went to Virginia, perhaps they would some day come back to Heacham to claim John's inheritance at the Hall.

So it was that a young Norfolk gentleman-farmer left his mother, his brothers and his village to undertake a journey that would lead him eventually into the arms of a Virginian Indian, the Princess Pocahontas. Her image greets visitors as they make their way into Heacham village today.

Heacham village sign by Becky R.

There is another reminder of the Princess Pocahontas in the North Aisle of Heacham Parish Church. The rather grumpy looking bust of the Princess tops the memorial erected in 1933 'to mark a picturesque episode in the history of two nations, by friends in England and America.

Pocahontas Memorial in Heacham Parish Church

3. Going to Virginia

Norfolk to London

As John and his young wife travelled down the rough road through King's Lynn and Cambridge on their way to London, they must have wondered what life would be like in the New World of Virginia. With John on horseback and his wife and all their belongings carried on a heavy cart, the week's journey would have provided plenty of opportunity to think of all the things they had forgotten to bring! What clothes would they need? What would the weather be like at Jamestown? What food supplies should they take, or would the Company provide them with food and shelter? Would they need farming tools to work the land and how would John cope with manual labour, having spent his youth in relative luxury at Heacham Hall? They must have known that they were taking a huge gamble, not just with their money but with their lives.

John Smith's 'True Relation' about the Jamestown Colony first published in 1608

The Virginia Company had done their best to hide the truth about what was happening in Virginia. They published glowing accounts of the wonderful nature of the place, of the friendliness of the Indians and the perfect climate. Virginia was said to be a 'heaven on earth' with great potential for supplying the gold that the Spanish had found so easily in Central and South America. The awful truth about the heat of the first two summers in Jamestown, the shortage of good drinking water and the diseases that had killed over half the first colonists was carefully concealed. Only 'good news' was to be sent back to London from the young colony and the official version was that they had made a good start amongst friendly Indians. The Virginia Company worked hard to keep the London investors interested in their project, helped by the printing in London of Captain John Smith's 1608 account of the colony. He had written it as a letter to a friend, not for publication, but the Company had it published, without his permission or knowledge!

A new charter for Virginia

In 1609, the Company petitioned King James I to grant them a new Charter, which was drafted by Sir Edmund Sandys, a very able organiser. His proposals provided for a new system of leadership. Under the first Charter, the Council members in Jamestown had elected a 'President' each year. But several Presidents had died before completing their term of office or had been deposed by the other Council members. Even the strongest leader, Captain John Smith, had found it difficult to hold the colony together when there was so much disagreement. The new Charter authorised the Company in London to appoint one leader, to be the Governor of the Colony, free to make decisions in Jamestown. He was to be advised by a Council of nominated leaders in Virginia but they could not over-rule the Governor. With this streamlined leadership, the Company hoped to stop the squabbling.

The Charter also expanded the Colony's territory to include the country to the south where Sir Walter Raleigh had tried but failed to establish a colony at Roanoke in the 1580s. To the west, there was no limit. The Charter simply said that the Colony ran to the 'western ocean', in other words, right across America to the Pacific. No-one, in London or in Virginia, had a clear idea how far this was! The English still thought of America as a narrow continent with the great Pacific Ocean not that far away beyond the hills to the west. How wrong they were!

The Company also decided to establish a new capital further up the James River at a place that was healthier than Jamestown. It was to be called Henricus, in honour of Henry, Prince of Wales, the eldest son of King James I of England.

To finance the new venture, the Treasurer, Sir Thomas Smythe, started vigorous fund-raising by selling more shares. Many of the London City Companies contributed large amounts of money. The churches added their support. With the possibility of good relations with the Indians, it was hoped that many of the Indians would become Christians. To the churches in London, it was important that these new converts should be Protestant members of the Church of England. Sermons were preached in London churches to encourage the faithful to invest in a new start for the Virginia colony.

Once sufficient funds were being received, the Company began to recruit leaders for the new venture. Sir Thomas Gates, a tough soldier and a veteran of the Dutch wars, was chosen as overall governor. The most experienced ship's captains and navigators were chosen to take the planned fleet of ships across the Atlantic. Sir George Somers had commanded naval expeditions against the Spanish in the West Indies for Elizabeth I. Although he was well over fifty and had retired from the sea to become the Member of

Parliament for Lyme Regis, he was persuaded to become the overall fleet commander.

Two of the Captains who had sailed with the first Virginia voyage joined the new venture, the one-armed Christopher Newport and John Ratcliffe who had been one of the first to serve as President at Jamestown. Two other former members of the Council, Archer and Martin, also signed on. Another very experienced sailor, Sir Samuel Argall, was sent ahead to find a more direct route across the Atlantic avoiding the need to call in at the Spanish West Indies. William Strachey, who had studied at Cambridge and at Gray's Inn as a lawyer, became the Secretary to the Colony.

The Company recruited Rev Richard Bucke to lead the colony in the ways of the Church of England as their Chaplain. All the members of the first Jamestown expedition had been men or boys. In their plan to re-establish the colony, the Company decided to send men, women and children with all their belongings, tools and farm animals, to establish a little England on the American shore.

Boarding the fleet

The Company signed on hundreds of skilled workmen with useful trades, carpenters and blacksmiths, hunters, fishermen and farmers. Those too poor or too unwilling to invest their own money could go as 'indentured servants' to work for the Company and be housed and fed, for a fixed number of years. When their service was completed, they would be given land to occupy and an opportunity to build their own futures. When not enough willing recruits could be found, the Company turned to the Lord Mayor and City Companies to pay for the homeless poor to be taken away from London, together with orphans from charities like Christ's Hospital. Those who threatened the peace of London were to be transported to a new life in the wilderness.

In June 1609, more than five hundred passengers, from every social group and from all over England, gathered at Blackwall on the north shore of the Thames to board the fleet of ships assembled by the Company. Among the gentry were a young gentleman-farmer and his wife from Heacham, Mr and Mrs John Rolfe. Mrs Rolfe was expecting their first child.

The *Sea Venture* by Dean R.

They boarded the *Sea Venture*, the 250 ton flagship of the fleet, and joined the 'better sort' in the crowded ship. There would have been little privacy and less comfort for the young Mrs Rolfe and she must have wondered where her husband was leading her.

On one of the smaller ships, probably amongst the riff-raff in the hold, was a fourteen-year-old boy from the Norfolk village of Congham, ten miles south of Heacham. Henry Spelman was the son or possibly the nephew of Sir Henry Spelman. It seems that young Henry had fallen out with his family and his village and decided to seek new adventures by running away to Virginia.

Shipwreck on the Devil's Islands

After they had cleared the English Channel, the first part of the voyage went well. Somers and Newport led the great fleet of eight ships down to the Canary Islands and then struck out due west across the empty ocean. They followed the old sailing route to the West Indies:

'Sail south until the butter melts and then head west.'

But by leaving England in June, they reached the Tropics at the hottest time of the year. Thirty two would-be colonists and sailors died in the heat. Two baby boys were born but sadly died. In late July, the hurricane season started in the Caribbean and on Monday July 24th, a great storm hit the fleet. Four of the ships ran on before the wind toward the American shore and reached Cape Henry at the mouth of Chesapeake Bay in early August. Three more limped into the Bay in the following days and weeks. Amongst the passengers was young Henry Spelman.

The flagship, the *Sea Venture*, and the small ship she was towing, disappeared to the north during the storm. For some inexplicable reason, the Company had allowed all the main leaders, Gates, Somers, Newport, Buck and Stracey to sail in one ship. With them was the only copy of the new Charter. Mr and Mrs John Rolfe of Heacham were amongst the terrified passengers on the *Sea Venture*.

Storm at Sea

'White horses roaring like lions ram and smash into the side of the ship, as our helpless Sea Venture is flung from side to side like a ball. The monstrous giants of the sea wreak havoc in their wake; they can swallow ships whole, ours is merely a mouthful. We ride their watery backs clinging on to their manes of watery death.

Wild Sea to the West, East, North and South !!! Our arch-enemy calls in reinforcements. They come surging over our ship. The hull begins to crack as one bursts through. WE'RE LOST!!

(by Jack C.)

As the *Sea Venture* hurtled north with all her sails in shreds and the hurricane howling through her rigging, the crew realised that her hull was splitting open to the sea. After four days of frantic baling and pumping by all on board, from Admiral Somers to the youngest passenger, the ship was barely afloat. As dawn broke through the racing clouds on the Friday morning, Somers saw land ahead. The surf was breaking on a jagged coral reef with a low island shore beyond. They were running onto the Devil's Islands, called that because so many ships had been wrecked on the reefs. The tiny cluster of rocks thrust up into the ocean five hundred miles from the American shore had another name which still brings fear to sailors even in our day. It was called

Bermuda, and lies at one corner of the infamous Bermuda triangle into which ships and planes have simply disappeared.

Safe on the Reef

Somers knew that if the ship ran onto the reef, she would break up and all aboard would be drowned. He saw that there was a narrow gap in the coral. He steered the *Sea Venture* towards it. If the ship got through into the calm of the lagoon beyond, or even if she could be wedged fast in the reef, the hull might hold together for a few more minutes. It might be long enough for them to use their boats to ferry all on board across the calm waters of the lagoon and onto the beach.

The ship hit the reef and was held in the grip of the coral but she did not sink. When the wind died down, the crew used the ship's boats to ferry all the passengers to the shore. All aboard were saved from what had seemed certain drowning. Timber, tools and whatever might be useful were salvaged from the wreck and brought on shore. Once safe, they discovered further blessings on these *'Devil's Islands'*. Although they were uninhabited, there were springs of good fresh water, plentiful tropical fruits and even herds of semi-wild pigs, the descendants of animals which had swum ashore from previous ship-wrecks. They were safe and they knew that they could survive on the Devil's Islands.

Getting to Virginia

Gates and Somers had been commissioned to take the party to Virginia, not to land them on the Devil's Islands and they were not going to give up easily. They sent one of the ship's boats with a crew of six to try to sail to Jamestown and to come back with help to rescue all the others on

Bermuda. The boat never returned. Perhaps they did reach the shore of America but the crew must have died before they could reach Jamestown. Somers decided that if no ship would come to rescue them, they would have to build their own vessel to get to Virginia. With timber and tools from the wreck of the *Sea Venture*, and whatever they could find on the island, four carpenters set about building not one sea-going ship but two.

Throughout that winter, the whole party kept healthy on the plentiful supply of pork, fish and fruit. Somers' cook fell in love with one of the other servants and the happy couple were married by Rev Bucke. He also christened two babies born on the island. Mr and Mrs John Rolfe had a daughter who was named Bermuda, with Captain Newport, William Stracey and Mrs Horton as godparents. By the end of April 1610, the 40-foot *Deliverance* and the 29-foot *Patience* were finished and ready to sail. Sadly, before they sailed, the Rofe's baby, Bermuda, died. She was buried on the island.

In early May, the survivors boarded the two small ships. Twelve days later, a westerly wind carried them into the mouth of Chesapeake Bay. Somewhere along the way, John Rolfe's young wife must have died as well as his daughter as there is no record of her ever living in Virginia.

After the party reached Jametown. William Stracey wrote an account of their Bermuda ship wreck and island adventure. His account reached London in 1611 and was widely read in England. The story is said to have provided William Shakespeare with the inspiration for his new play, *The Tempest*.

> **The Tempest by William Shakespeare** *(Act 1 Scene 2)*
>
> Prospero: Of the king's ship,
>   The mariners, say how thou hast dispos'd,
>   And all the rest o' the fleet?
>
> Ariel: Safely in harbour
>   Is the king's ship; in the deep nook, where once
>   Thou call'dst me up at midnight to fetch dew
>   From the still-vex'd Bermoothes, there she's hid;
>   The mariners all under hatches stowed,
>   Who, with a charm join'd to their suff'red labour,
>   I have left asleep; and for the rest o' th' fleet,
>   Which I dispers'd, they all have met again,....
>
> (first perfomed in 1611, at the Globe Theatre, London)

The play opens with a ship at sea, in grave danger of sinking and being swept onto rocks. Lightning strikes the masts and St Elmo's fire flashes through the rigging, before she is miraculously saved in a *'deep nook'*. All aboard escape with their lives onto an *'uninhabited island'*. Although the play also refers to 'Milan' and 'Naples', there is a direct references to *'the still-vex'd Bermoothes'* as the links with Stracey's account become clear.

Return to Jamestown

When Gates and Somers brought their two tiny ships up the James River to Jamestown Colony, nothing could have prepared them for what they found.

The first four ships carrying Ratcliffe, Archer, Martin and the main party had survived the storm and reached Jamestown in August 1609. The other three ships limped in over the next month, while Smith was still completing his year as President of the Colony. Argall's ship had arrived earlier and he had warned Smith of the change to the Charter. Faced with so many old enemies among the new arrivals who claimed that there was a new Governor sent to take over his powers as President, Smith had asked for evidence of the new arrangements, stating that until the new Charter arrived, he was remaining in control under the terms of the old one.

They reluctantly agreed, but the colony was soon in trouble again. With inadequate stores to feed so many, Smith dispersed the new colonists to live off the land in separate settlements, some at the mouth of the river, others higher up at the river falls. Struggling to maintain control over these scattered and disgruntled groups, Smith handed over his Presidency to Martin, who promptly handed it back. The Norfolk boy, Henry Spelman, was sent to live with the Indians as a token of good faith between the English and Powhatan, effectively a hostage in an arrangement which was commonly used to seal an agreement between two groups. He later claimed that Smith had 'sold' him to the Indians. Whatever really happened, this arrangement probably saved Spelman's life.

With authority slipping from his grasp, Smith returned to Jamestown and on the way suffered an accident, or was it an accident? His gunpowder pouch, hanging from his belt and lying in his lap as he lay asleep in the boat, caught fire and exploded. In agony and with a deep wound in his thigh, Smith jumped overboard to put out the fire. They fished him out of the river and took him back to Jamestown.

Although Smith survived, his terrible burns forced him to sail home as soon as he could. He left the Colony with the weak George Percy as President. Powhatan now knew that the English, with many women and children amongst the new settlers, were planning to stay. Jamestown was to be a permanent settlement. Powhatan also knew that the English could not grow enough food for themselves. He ordered all the peoples under his control to refuse to trade in corn with the English. He also decided to weaken them further by harassing each settlement as much as he could.

The English are killed and the survivors starve

Powhatan sent Henry Spelman to Jamestown fort with a message which seemed friendly enough. It was an invitation to visit him to trade for part of the Indian's harvest of corn. Ratcliffe and many of his men set out by ship to take up the offer but it was a trap. John Smith had always exchanged hostages with the Indians at the start of any major negotiation, but Ratcliffe took no such precaution.

The English were welcomed to the Indians' village and invited to stay overnight. In the morning, they began to trade for corn. When the English realised that they were being cheated by the Indians pushing up the base of each straw basket and so giving short measure, a dispute broke out which soon developed into fighting. The English were scattered and killed in ones and twos, with Ratcliffe captured alive. It would have been better for him if he had been killed in the fighting. The Indians tied him to a stake in front of a large fire, surrounded by women. Very slowly, with much shouting and dancing, the women began to cut the skin from Radlciffe's flesh. They used mussel shells as knives and then burnt the bloody strips in the fire. Eventually, they burnt the screaming Ratcliffe at the stake. Henry Spelman was a witness of this atrocity and was one of the few to escape when the Indians attacked the English who had stayed on the ship.

Frances West, another of the gentlemen amongst the new arrivals, then attempted to trade with a group of Indians further away from the colony called the Patawomacks. They were less hostile to the English and not under Powhatan's control. President Percy sent West on what was intended to be the first of many successful trading expeditions. But rather than trading peacefully with them, West's soldiers shot several of the Indians and then forced the rest to load his ship with corn. West then sailed his ship straight out to sea and home to England. Not only had he deprived the colonists at Jamestown of their last hope of food, he had made enemies of the only people still prepared to trade with the English.

As hunger gnawed at those left in Jamestown, some tried to steal food from the store. They were caught and hanged. Others tried to creep out into the surrounding forest to scavenge for roots, snakes and squirrels, anything they could find to eat. Most of them were caught and killed by the Indians. Ravenous men chewed the leather of their boots and even sucked the starch which they had used as stiffening out of their ruffs and collars.

Finally, starvation drove them to eat each other. In the depth of the winter of 1609-1610, bodies were dug out of the frozen ground, English and Indian, and were eaten. Recent excavations at Jamestown by the Jamestown Rediscovery project have found a human skull and human bones with the marks of knives across them. They have been identified as the bones of a young English woman, who they have named '*Jane*'. Her bones provide gruesome evidence of the truth of the reports of canibalism at Jamestown during this terrible 'starving time'.

Evacuating Jamestown

Some of the English survived, among them George Percy still President of the Jamestown Colony. In March 1610, he raised sufficient energy to visit the settlement based at Point Comfort at the mouth of the river James. To his amazement, he found them fit and well fed. They had come through the winter by eating shell-fish and their own pigs, unaware of the horrors of life at the fort not more than fifty miles upstream. Percy was still at Point Comfort when the two tiny ships in which Gates and Somers had brought the survivors from Bermuda, finally arrived in Virginia

At last the Colony had its new leadership and new Charter, as Gates and Somers sailed up the James River in May 1610. Two days later, they reached the remains of what was left of Jamestown. Of the five hundred men, women and children who had sailed from England in the great fleet under the new Charter, over four hundred had died of starvation and disease. Gates and Somers had little to offer the survivors. The food they had brought for their journey from Bermuda was almost finished.

Gates decided that the inevitable had to be faced. They would have to abandon the colony. The small ships were loaded with the survivors and anything still useful from the colony. They buried the guns from the fort and, to the joy of those still alive, set off back down the James River leaving the remains of the fort at the settlement intact in case it was needed to be re-established at some future date.

4. Powhatan's daughter - the girl with many names

While John Rolfe was growing up in Norfolk, on the other side of the Atlantic Ocean in the land the English called Virginia, a woman of the Algonquian speaking people was giving birth. Around her in the darkness of the longhouse, the older women encouraged her to think of the new life to come, new life given by the great Creating Spirit, Ahone. Outside in the village of Werowocomoco, home of the great chief Powhatan, the shaman priests danced and sang to keep Okeus, the spirit of thunder, well away from the birth.

The child was a girl. Her father whispered a secret name into her ear, Matoaka. Her mother and the people of the village called her Amonute. Powhatan had many wives and Matoaka was just one of many sons and daughters. His name came from the village by the great river where he had been born many years before, but his own people called him Wahunsonacock. He was a tall, strong man who could strike fear into the hearts of even the bravest of his people.

From the blue mountain ridges to the west to the mouth of Chesapeake Bay where the rivers ran into the great sea, the people all recognised Powhatan as their overlord or Werowance. Every year, after their harvest, they brought him his share of their corn as tribute. He ruled over a great empire of Algonquian speaking peoples, more than thirty separate groups living in the forests along the banks of the rivers of the Chesapeake. Some of these people he had conquered in war, others had agreed to join forces with him to resist their enemies to the west and to the north.

Powhatan's people called their land of rivers and forests, *Tsenacomoco*, which means 'our home'. To them it was the centre of the world, a sacred land which gave them all that they needed.

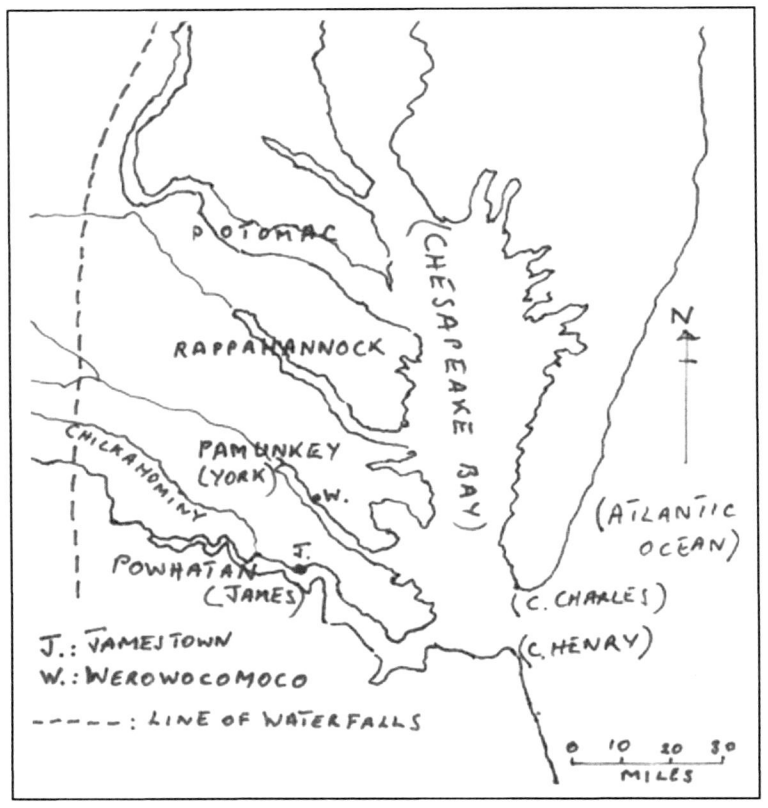

Sketch map of Tsenacomoco with Algonquian names of rivers and English names in brackets

Living in Tsenacomoco

Powhatan's people lived in small villages, clusters of houses around a central fire. Each village was close to one of the great rivers which gave each group its name. The Chickahominy lived along the river which ran into the great river which the English called the James. The Pamunkey lived along the river of that name to the north. The English called this river, the York. Further north, lay the territory of the Mattaponi. Each people had their own Werowance or chief, although this was often one of Powhatan's relatives so that he could keep control over them. We do not know which of the many tribes gave a young woman to Powhatan as one of his many wives. That young woman gave him a daughter called, Amonute, but her mother may have been a member of the Pamunkey, the Rappahannocks or any one of the many peoples who made up Powhatan's confederacy. We only know that it was Amonute who grew up to be Pocahontas.

But we do know about her people, from the writing of Henry Spelman. He was placed with Powhatan's people byJohn Smith to live amongst them as part of an agreement between the two peoples. We also still have the pictures brought back to England by the artist-governor of the failed Roanoke colony, just to the south. These water-colour paintings have been preserved in the British Library and provide a vivid set of illustrations of what living in an Algonquian community was like in the late 16th and early 17th Century.

Celebration

The wedding was celebrated with wild dancing and a great feast. They made music with reed pipes, drums and rattles of dried gourds. The girls and boys dressed up just like their parents, painting their bodies and wearing necklaces and bracelets made out of shells and animal bones. They also celebrated when young teenaged boys went through a nine-month ordeal of physical hardship, isolation and fasting, after which some were picked to be leaders.

(by Francesca M.)

These pictures, and the picture of a village below, are from the paintings of John White who recorded images of Algonquian villages, women and men in the 1590s.

Amonute's home

Amonute's village was really hot, so hot that little children ran around naked especially in the summer time. The women were very muscular and strong because they had to do all the work. They had to collect water from the river, food from the fields, dig in the fields, prepare animal skins to make clothes, and make fires.

The men had long hair and had to shave the hair from one side of their heads so that when they were shooting arrows their hair would not get caught in their bow strings.
(by Emma)

As was the custom amongst the Algonquian speaking Indians soon after the child of a great chief was born, Amonute and her mother and child were sent away from Powhatan's village at Werowocomoco to spend her childhood amongst her mother's people. We do not know which of the Virginian tribes her mother came from but it could have been the Rappahannocks who lived beside the river which still has that name.

Before her first birthday, Powhatan sent his warriors to attack the Kecoughtans, living at the mouth of the Powhatan River to bring them into his empire. Only the

Monahans of the western hills, and the Susquahennas, tall and fierce warriors to the north, held out against him.

Women and Men

As she grew up, Amonute learned the skills of her people, the Powhatans. The women and the children had to gather nuts and fruit, roots and other plants. They cooked over outdoor fire pits and made soups and stews in large clay pots over the fire. Sometimes they added meat or fish to the stew.

They made bread with the flour that had been ground from seeds collected from the forest, acorns, walnuts and chestnuts, or from the corn which they grew in gardens near to their houses. Women and children cared for these gardens using tools made from bone and wood for weeding and digging To preserve their food for use in the winter when food was scarce, they would smoke it over the fire. The women did not waste any part of a deer, as they would make clothing out of its hide, after it had been scraped and tanned in order to soften it.

Powhatan men hunted geese, swans, wild turkeys, rabbits, squirrels and larger animals like deer and bear. In the spring they used nets and spears to catch large quantities of fish. Oyster and scallop shells were made into tools and jewellery. Men would spend their time in the villages making and repairing their tools and weapons, their tomahawks and bows and arrows. Stones were made into axes for chopping and cutting, and flaked into arrow and spear points for hunting. Deer provided meat as well as skins for clothing, bones for tools and weapons, and sinews for fastening tool and weapon parts. Boys played in scarecrow houses standing in the middle of fields, throwing missiles at rabbits and racoons which might nibble at the crops.

(by Jade S.)

The villages in which the people lived were not permanent settlements. They lived in *'yekakins'*, temporary longhouses made of bent saplings covered with mats and skins. When the land around the village became less fertile, the people would move to a new place in the forest. The Powhatans had no iron tools so clearing new land for a garden was very hard work. Once the land was cleared, they would sow beans and maize together in mounds and when the harvest was ready they would eat a feast outside, with singing and dancing around the great fire. They would store the spare food from a good harvest in thatched graneries raised above the gound.

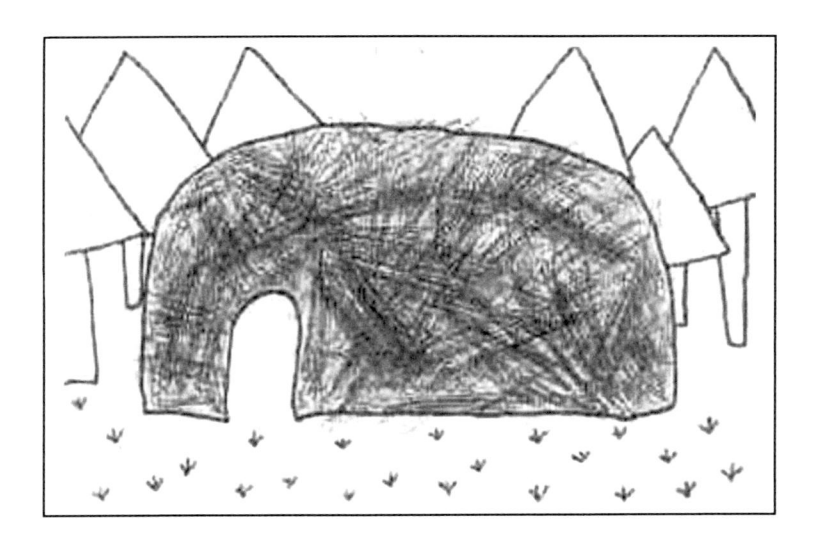

Powhatans' longhouse or 'yekakin' by Laura T.

'Just a normal day'

Men are burning tree trunks into canoes,
Sharpening arrows and spear heads
Then shooting the arrows at deer, rabbits and turkeys.
Women are skinning the deer for coats,
And making mats for the walls of houses.
Children are practising with bows & arrows.
It's just a normal day in Tsenacomoco.

(by Chris R.)

The coming of the white-skins

There had been visitors to this land of rivers and forest in Powhatan's lifetime. A Spanish ship had come into the great bay and made contact with the people, trying to introduce a new God to them. The Spanish had been chased away, taking with them captives who were never seen again. Powhatan's shamans who had the power to see into the future warned him that others would come from the sea and take his land. He felt threatened by this news and attacked the people who lived on the shore of the great sea, the Chesapeakes. Soon all of them, men, women and children were wiped out.

When she was ten, Amonute was sent back to Powhatan's village at Werowocomoco to learn the ways of leaders of her people but she was still a child. In the heat of summer, she still ran naked with her half-brothers and half-sisters. They played at hunting with flint-tipped arrows and fishing in the river. Powhatan noticed the child with her bright eyes and inquisitive spirit. She was respectful of the elders, but not afraid to ask them questions. He gave her a new name, Pocahontas, 'the playful one', and she became his favourite daughter.

Pocahontas was at Werowocomoco, when news came of three great ships in the bay. The flags on their ships were not the same as the flags on the Spanish ships that came before. Men came ashore. At first they had been welcomed by the chief of the Kecoughtan people, who was a son of Powhatan. But the Kecoughtan had then attacked the white-skins and they returned to their ships to sail on up the great river. When they reached the mouth of the Chickahominy river, they came ashore again, to be met in turn by the chief of the Paspahegh, who gave them food. But he also told them that they were not welcome. They clearly did not understand. Further up the great river, the chief of the Appomatocs met them with his warriors. Their warlike attitude was intended to drive away the white-skins and they sailed back down the river.

On the north bank, there was a low-lying island which the Paspahegh had used for hunting. They had abandoned it before the white-skins came. It was plagued with biting insects and the soil was poor for planting crops. But the newcomers stopped there and tied their ships to trees. On the next day, the chief of the Paspahegh went to the island with many warriors, enough to outnumber the white-skins. He invited them to lay down their arms and join in a feast. But one of his men picked up an iron hatchet. When the newcomers tried to take it from him, fighting started and would have developed into a battle, but the chief of the Paspahegh called his men together and stalked off to find a better time to attack these strangers who had come into their land.

Powhatan's people prepare to attack.

When the white-skins landed on the shore, they were armed with shooting sticks, shovels and axes. We were watching them from behind the trees. We raised our arrows and aimed, preparing for whatever could happen to us on that day.

"Should we fire our arrows at the intruders?" one of our men whispered with anger in his voice. "No! We have hardly any men. If they should want war, we would surely lose." So it was decided that we would gather men that night, but attack when the sun was above the trees.

Whilst the white-skins were cutting some trees down and making them into a fort, we were gathering our greatest and fiercest warriors. After we had assembled, we sharpened our weapons, as we prepared for battle against the strangers, Soon it would be time for the battle, one that would be remembered for ever. *(by Josh S)*

Powhatan warrior by Rosie

The opportunity soon came. The strangers sent many of their men further up the river in boats, leaving some to guard the island and their ships. The Paspahegh attacked and would have overwhelmed the strangers when a great gun was fired from one of the ships. The terrified warriors ran for their lives. When the strangers who had been up the river returned, they started to build a fort to make a better defence of the island. They set tree trunks on end in the earth to form the walls of their fort and stayed inside these walls. From that time onwards, the strangers and the Paspahegh did not trust each other.

English musketeer by Thomas L.

The English attack first

The Indians are getting close to our fort again. We can hear lots of noises and we saw some signs, we can hear low whistling; arrows are going now. One of our boats disappeared last night; a sentry went missing as well. One soldier said, about two days later, noises were growing louder from the savages' camp. We got ready as they warned us that they were coming. The captain got us all in order as we had a plan to attack their village before they attacked us.

Next morning we were divided into twenties and we attacked. It was difficult to load our muskets as they are very slow to reload. When the attack was finished, we had lost twenty men to the savages but many more of them were killed.

(Rebecca M.)

Watching the white-skins by Josh D.

As they watched the white-skins, the Paspahegh were puzzled. All were men or boys and they wore thick coats. Some wore shirts of iron with iron covers on their heads. They seemed to have no interest in planting crops and had little skill in hunting deer and catching fish. After the season of planting corn, two of the ships sailed down the river and out to sea. Many of the white-skins were left behind on the island with one small ship. As they had no fields, they would have no harvest and they began to offer hatchets, copper and beads to the Paspahegh in exchange for corn. As the summer heat got stronger, the men in the fort on the island moved less and less. Even those who were active seemed to be very few in number. Outside the fort, the people watched and waited.

Meeting the English Werowance

One of the white-skins, a short bearded man who had learnt some words of their language, told the Paspahegh who came with food to trade that they were English and that he was their Werowance or 'Captain'. All the trading should be with him. Gradually, the Paspahegh came to trust this man, finding that he drove a hard bargain but did not try to cheat them. He told them that his name was John Smith

When autumn came to the rivers and the trees turned to red and gold, this man set out from the island with other English to trade further up the river. They explored the James river and then sailed up the Chickahominy.

The capture of the English Werowance

In the winter, the chief of the white-skin savages, the man called John Smith, set out into the river country. He wasn't alone; there were seven other savages with him. We kept on tracking them and the chief white-skin was captured by our braves. He was led on a six-mile walk to our village.

We kept him secure and guarded in a hut. He was taken to meet chief Powhatan. This was the first white-skin ever to meet our great chief. A great feast took place and

then two blocks of stone where placed together and the white-skin's head placed on them. We were going to execute him by our usual means; death by beating of the brains.

Then, suddenly, the chief's daughter, Pocahontas, ran out and covered the man's head with her body. He could not be killed without Powhatan's daughter being grievously injured. After pleading with her father, Pocahontas persuaded him to spare the white-skin's life. Our chief and the white-skins made an agreement. We would supply them with food and they would supply us with their powerful weapons, which can kill enemies instantly. Our two peoples were joined in friendship from that day

(by Ruth E.)

Trading for food

The English on their island were now completely dependent on the food received from Powhatan's people. But after John Smith returned to the island, the people saw the tall masts of another ship coming up the river. The English Werowance with one arm had returned with sixty more men and more supplies, the same man who had first brought the English to the river. Not long after they landed and joined the small group of English on the island, a great fire started in the thatched roofs of the houses and the whole village burnt to the ground. Despite this set-back, the English built their houses again and began again to trade for food.

The English always seemed to be hungry. Perhaps it was because they had no women with them to plant crops and did not know how to plant for themselves. Perhaps it was because the English spent so much time searching the area for a substance they called 'gold'. Pocahontas was curious. She visited Jamestown many times and played with the English boys, just as she would play with the children at Werowocomoco. Pocahontas ran races with them around the fort, hid in the houses and practised cart-wheels in the open spaces. The English were amused that this naked girl seemed to enjoy playing at the Island so much. The man they called Smith taught her some words of the English language and she taught him how to speak her language, Algonquian, although few others amongst the English showed any interest in what she and the other Indians said. She would often bring gifts to the fort, corn or venison, food to keep the colony alive. Her father smiled at her kindness.

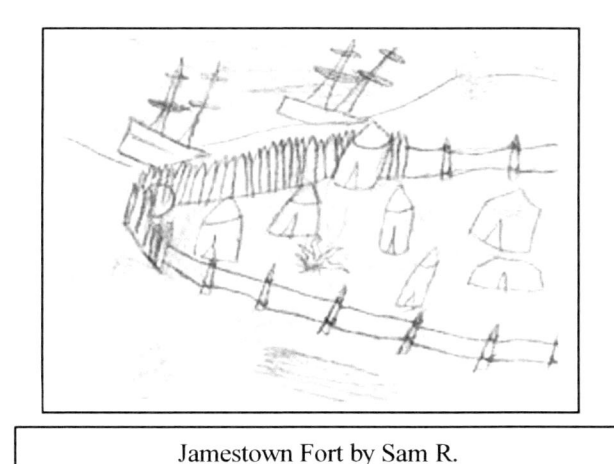

Jamestown Fort by Sam R.

But there was conflict as well as friendship. The English captured people of the Paspahegh who, they claimed, had been stealing. After yet more English men arrived on yet another ship, Powhatan's men captured two of them as they searched for food in the woods. He sent a message to the fort that he would exchange these captives for the people held by the English. This was the custom between the Powhatans and their neighbours. But Smith set out from

Jamestown with many soldiers, and attacked the nearest villages, burning the houses and breaking up their dug-out canoes. Powhatan returned the two English prisoners but he did not forget his anger at the English attack.

After the heat of the summer had eased a little and the corn had been harvested, the tall ship came back for a third time with more of the English. Amongst them were two women. Perhaps the English were planning to stay on their island. Their one-armed chief brought gifts for Powhatan from a great king beyond the seas. He gave the chief a metal ring to put on his head, as a token of this great king's friendship. Powhatan was not impressed by the metal ring, although he gave the English his decorated cloak and an old pair of shoes in exchange. He much preferred the small white dog that John Smith gave him as another present from the great king. Dogs were useful for hunting and could be eaten when the corn had all gone in the middle of winter.

The hungry English

The English were still hungry. They traded for corn with the Nansemond people and even came to Powhatan's village to trade. This so angered the great chief that he decided to kill Smith and his companions. Once again, Pocahontas intervened. Although she was terrified that Powhatan would find out, she came to the English in the night and warned Smith of the plan to kill them all. He tried to reward her with beads, which filled her heart with sorrow as the beads would have given her away to her father. So she refused to accept them. John Smith realised his mistake and the English escaped before the attack came.

At about this time, the people who lived near to the Island noticed a change in the activity at the fort. It was as if the English had awakened from a great sleep. No longer did they wait each day to receive their food from the store. Men started to clear trees and plant gardens. New houses were built for all to shelter in. It was more difficult to steal hatchets and swords from them as the English posted guards at the entrance to the island.

But there was another change as well. The English could be seen running around the fort trying to catch animals which the people had not seen before. They had fur like mice and long whiskers and naked tails. They were larger than mice but smaller than rabbits. The English called them rats. They had been brought by the English in their ships and escaped onto the land. They were eating all the corn that the English had traded.

The people had already taught the English how to grow corn, beans and pumpkins, and leaves for smoking called tobacco. Now they showed them how to survive when the rains failed and the crops did not grow. There were many dry summers at that time. When the corn shrivelled up in the heat, the people dug up the roots of a plant which they called 'tuckahoe'. They found it growing in marshy places and although it was not as good to eat as corn and beans, it would at least keep them alive. The English did not know about 'tuckahoe' but the people showed them..

In really bad years, the people would move to the shores of the great rivers and eat what they could find, crabs and shell-fish like mussels and oysters. These were not as good to eat as deer and turkeys but again enough to keep them all alive. When the corn ran out again, John Smith sent the English to live in smaller groups away from the Island to find food for themselves. When the spring came and the rivers were full of fish coming up to spawn, the English could catch them and grow fat again.

After the third summer of the English coming, the tall ships came into the bay again, not just one, but many of them. They brought many men and women and even some small English children. Some of these newcomers stayed on the island but others moved to the mouth of the river and to other places up towards the great falls, where the river pours over the rocks. Powhatan was now sure that the English had come to take all of his land. His people watched as John Smith travelled between the different groups. Some lived in peace but others attacked the people living close to them. Powhatan heard that John Smith had been in a boat travelling back to the island when he had been injured by a great fire in the powder bag which he carried.

'The Englishman is dead'

John Smith's body was badly burnt and the English did not expect him to live. He was still alive when his boat reached Jamestown but in great pain. Perhaps one of the English in the boat had tried to kill him. Powhatan knew that John Smith had made many enemies amongst the English. Some were saying that he would be sent away accused of great crimes. They said that he had plotted the death of the leaders of the English with Powhatan and his people. Others said that John Smith had tried to make himself king in Powhatan's place by marrying Pocahontas, his favourite daughter. Powhatan laughed when he heard this because he knew that his people would never agree to his power being passed on to one of his children. Their custom was to find a successor amongst the brothers of the Werowance, not the children, but the English did not understand this.

John Smith was seen to be alive when they took him onto the great ship. But the ship did not sail for two weeks and Powhatan's people were told that John Smith had died. When Powhatan himself heard, he knew that the peace and friendship he had agreed with John Smith and, through him with the English, must now come to an end. The message that the Englishman was dead was taken to Pocahontas. Never again would she be able to visit her friend. She must forget the English.

Pocahontas was very sad when she was told that Captain John Smith was dead. All she could think about was her friendship with him. Everybody was comforting her; she was glad that she still had her family and friends around her. Every day she walked far around the forest thinking, talking to herself and singing about her friend Captain John Smith. *(by Helen D.)*

Pocahontas' river

'This is my river, the river my people call Rappahannock, surrounded by deep forests, rich with all the food we need in all seasons. My river runs by a sandy shore and underneath a black, rocky cliff. My land is full of beautiful wild trees and plants. In amongst these plants are deer, turkeys and many other animals. In the running river, there is much life too, otters and fish, swimming freely with the current. Brown and black bears travel down to catch food, and drink the pale, blue water. My river lives in harmony with nature. I have walked upon the golden shore of Rappahannock many times. I have drifted down the river in my hollowed out canoe; I love the pale, blue water and all the creatures I see on my way.'

(by Tessa C.)

Soon she would be a child no longer. She would join the house of the women and begin to cover herself with skirts and cloaks like all the women of her people. It was the time for her to be given in marriage to one of her own. So Powhatan chose Kocoum, a brave warrior of the Rappahannock people. Pocahontas left her father's village and was taken to the long-house of Kocoum. Whether these two were happy together is not known, and there is no record of a child. Perhaps he found the 'Playful One' too disobedient to be a good wife for him. Some believe that he grew tired of her and sent her back to live with her father.

5. Mr and Mrs John Rolfe

Starting again

The disheartened Jamestown settlers, including John Rolfe, sailed down the James River on their way home to England. Or so they thought. To their amazement a small boat was spotted coming up the river with just one man on board. It was an English sailor with a letter addressed to 'Sir Thomas Gates, Governor of Virginia', ordering Sir Thomas to lead the colonists back to Jamestown. The letter was written by Thomas West, Lord Delaware. He had been appointed by the London Council to take over from Gates as Governor of Virginia. Gates turned the boats round and they sailed back up-river to Jamestown.

In April 1610, about a month before Gates and Somers set out from Bermuda, Lord Delaware had sailed from London with a fleet of three ships piloted by Samuel Argall on the new direct route to Jamestown. The fleet also brought supplies and a hundred and fifty new colonists, enough to replace those who were believed to have been lost with the *Sea Venture*. If Argall had not cut the voyage time to nine weeks and two days, the new Governor would have reached Virginia too late to stop the abandonment of Jamestown. As it was, when Delaware reached the site of the colony, he was so appalled by what he saw that he refused to go ashore until the stinking mess of the fort and settlement had been cleared up.

The new Governor

Lord Delaware brought enough food to last everyone for a year. The colony now had a wealth of leadership, Gates, Somers and Newport from Bermuda and Percy and Davis from Point Comfort. They were sworn in as the advisory Council. The lack of fresh meat led Somers and Argall to volunteer to return to Bermuda to collect a cargo of pork. Their two ships became separated on the way. Somers reached Bermuda but died there, apparently from eating too much of the pork that he had come to get. Argall went off to fish the rich cod banks of Newfoundland, eventually making his way back to Jamestown.

Delaware next decided to re-open contact with Powhatan who had still not lifted his ban on trading with the English. There had been minor skirmishes with the new settlers and it was time to teach Powhatan a lesson. A message was sent that all weapons and tools stolen by the Indians were to be returned and Powhatan's subjects must stop harassing the English. If this was ignored, the new Governor would declare a state of war. Powhatan's response was equally demanding. Either the English must leave altogether or confine themselves to Jamestown Island. If they still persisted in occupying other areas, he would attack the English settlements with his people's overwhelming numbers. By way of an additional demand, Powhatan asked his

Lordship to send him a coach and horses, as he understood that great lords in England used such a coach to visit each other.

Delaware was not amused. One of two Indians who had been caught stealing was punished by cutting off his hand and sent back to Powhatan. With him went the message repeating the English demands and warning that the next stage would be the burning of the Indians' crops. Percy was ordered to attack the nearest Paspahegh and Chickahominy villages. Fifteen Indians were killed, their queen and her children captured, villages burnt down and fields of corn destroyed. All this by people who, not many months before, had been dependent on the Indians for food! On the way back to Jamestown with the captive Queen and her children, the soldiers decided to throw the children into the river and shoot at their heads. When Lord Delaware was informed by Davis that the Queen was still alive, the Governor ordered Davis to burn her at the stake. Percy thought this a needless cruelty and ordered Davis to put her to the sword.

The Governor goes home

Lord Delaware, the Governor, was not a healthy man. He had been barely ten months at Jamestown when he suffered a series of illnesses. To make matters worse for him, sporadic warfare developed between Powhatan and the colony. In March 1611, he decided to hand the Governorship back to George Percy before boarding Captain Argall's ship to be taken back to England. Percy was once again left to sort out the mess. His response was to dress up in the magnificent clothes sent out by his brother and to prepare for war. The killing of the Paspahegh Queen and her children had broken one of the Indians' rules of war. The wives of chiefs and their children were never killed. Rather they were captured and held by the conqueror to ensure the good behaviour of the conquered.

Percy was not in charge for long. The Virginia Company in London were well aware of Lord Delaware's frailty. They had already decided to send a fitter Governor to lead the colony and to find a better site for the permanent settlement than the low-lying Jamestown Island. They chose Sir Thomas Dale, yet another veteran of the Dutch wars. He like Gates was a mercenary employed by the Dutch when James I came to the throne. Returning to London to get married in 1611, he was granted five years leave of absence from his Dutch contract to work for the Virginia Company, as 'Marshal and Deputy Governor'. Dale swept into Virginia like an avenging angel, determined to bring the unruly rabble, English and Indian, under the harshest of military discipline.

With Dale came a new chaplain, the gentle Cambridge-educated Puritan, Rev Alexander Whittacker. He believed that he had been called by God to bring the gospel to the Virginian Indians. Between them, they were to put the colony on a much firmer footing.

Martial law

Dale first announced that Jamestown and all the other settlements were subjected to a new set of *'Lawes Divine, Morall and Martiall'*. It was a terrible code of law. Execution, by hanging, shooting, breaking on the wheel or burning at the stake became the punishment for even the most minor crimes such as thefts from another settler's garden, unauthorised trading with the Indians, adultery or running away under attack. Those who tried to steal food from the store were tied to trees and starved to death. The Colony's day began and ended with the beating of the drum to call the colonists together. Anyone late was whipped, as was anyone caught '*doing the necessities of nature*' within a quarter of a mile of the fort. Those who tried to escape from Jamestown were caught and executed. As Percy put it, '*all these extreme and cruel tortures, he used to terrify the rest*'.

Food was still short and Dale organised the planting of crops at Jamestown to ensure that some food was grown. He travelled seventy miles up the James river and found a better site for his new capital, where the River flowed in a great loop around a high bluff of fertile land. This was to be the site of the new *'citie of Henricus'*.

Dale took three hundred and fifty men including Whittacker and John Rolfe to this new site, and in ten days erected a stockade to enclose seven acres of land. The new township was soon completed with watch towers, a timber church, stores and houses for families to live in.

Houses at Henricus Citie by Megan C.

Dale then enclosed more land to the west and defended it with five fortified houses. One was Rock Hall, the vicarage for Alexander Whittacker, and another, Mount Malady, the first hospital built by the English in America. Sir Thomas Dale made his report to King James in London.

Letter to King James from Henricus Citie

Your Majesty,

We have arrived in Virginia, undergoing the most awful hardships and deprivations known to man along the way. Nonetheless, the Lord has, in His mercy, spared us for the purpose of increasing the glory of Your Gracious Majesty. I have taken the men to Henricus, named in honour of your son, Prince Henry to build a new Citie. We have set up camp under the most trying conditions, in fear of attack, indeed, in constant fear of our lives. The foul, filthy, treacherou, Indians are attacking at the very moment I am writing this important letter. The tide of battle works in our favour at the moment - God is indeed on the side of the Righteous. Our men are shooting (and hopefully killing) a great number of Savages. Nay – but our gravest hardship, sire, of this wild, uncivilised country is that the food is rapidly rotting into mouldy green and yellow. At least there is fresh water here, not like at Jamestown, save that which we must risk our lives to fetch it until we have a well within the citie. At least half of our exhausted men are lying on their beds. Eleven have died already – may God Bless their Eternal Souls..

Your loyal servant   Sir Thomas Dale

(by Laura)

Trading again with the Indians

Next, Powhatan's ban on trading with the colonists was undermined when they re-established the friendship of the Patawomacks. These people who lived on the Potomac River to the north had sold corn to Francis West. When Captain Argall returned from taking Lord Delaware back to England, he sailed up the Potomac and met with the Patawomacks. They decided to co-operate with the English and supplied Argall with a cargo of corn. Then Argall heard of an even bigger prize.

A young woman, Pocahontas, Powhatan's daughter had not been seen at Jamestown since the departure of Captain John Smith. There was a report that she was living with the Patawomacks. Argall decided to try to kidnap her and to use her as a hostage in his negotiations with Powhatan.

Pocahontas on board

His opportunity came in 1613. Sailing back to the Potomac, he made contact with the local Werowance, Japazeus. Argall told him that if their friendship was going to develop, Japazeus must betray Pocahontas to the English. The Werowance did not want to anger Powhatan, but was assured that Argall intended to treat the girl well. He also promised to protect the Patawomacks from Powhatan. Argall tempted Japazeus with another promise, the gift of a fine copper kettle, if he could persuade Pocahontas to come on board Argall's ship.

Argall used Japazeus' wife to persuade Pocahontas to board his ship. She agreed to go. The whole party spent the night on board and by the time Pocahontas discovered that she was a prisoner, it was too late. Japazeus and his wife, with their new kettle, went ashore and the ship sailed with Pocahontas on board. Captain Argall took Pocahontas to Jamestown. There she was treated as an honoured guest. The English were sure that with Pocahontas under their control, they could bring back friendship between Powhatan and the English.

Argall sent a message to Powhatan. If he wished to see his daughter again, he had to release all the English prisoners he had captured and return all the tools and weapons his people had stolen from Jamestown. Powhatan replied with a plea to Argall to treat his daughter well and an invitation to meet him on the Pamunkey River where the prisoners and the tools and weapons would be handed over. Powhatan waited but no word came from Argall. So the Werowance released some of the English prisoners and sent a few tools to Jamestown with a canoe full of corn. Both sides were using Pocahontas as a pawn in their attempts to control the other.

'The white-skins captured me on June 4th 1613. They wanted to trade me for English prisoners and weapons. But I grew to love being with the English, especially the time spent living with the Reverend. I used to ask him about God and how the world was made. He made me see how wonderful God was, so that while I was there, I wanted to be baptised as a Christian.

Every Sunday, I went to church to listen to the Reverend and sing hymns to the glory of God, and it was during one of my visits to church that I first noticed a handsome young man. I discovered that he was called John Rolfe'.

(by Ashleigh E.)

Good news to England

Dale sent a message on the next ship to England with the good news of the capture of Pocahontas. At last the English had the means to negotiate with Powhatan on their own terms. At Jamestown, they waited for his reply but none came. It seemed that Powhatan had lost interest in the release of his daughter. Dale took Pocahontas to Henricus where the Chaplain, Alexander Whittacker, was given the task of looking after her.

Rev Whittaker instructing Pocahontas, from the window in Willoughby Church

She was held prisoner at his house, Rock Hall. Whittacker found that she already spoke some English and encouraged her to learn more while developing her interest in the Christian faith. Pocahontas became his first opportunity to preach to an Indian, literally, to a captive audience.

One of the wives of the settlers was recruited to teach this Algonquian Princess the manners of a English lady and how to conduct herself in polite society. Nearby in the Henricus settlement, the young Norfolk widower, John Rolfe had established his own farm and was experimenting with new varieties of tobacco.

Sweet leaf

Even before he left England as a young man, Rolfe probably took up smoking. Tobacco from Spain and the West Indies was available in England from about 1580, and had been made popular by both Sir Walter Raleigh and Sir Francis Drake. By the early 1600s, people believed that tobacco was an effective cure for many illnesses. It was used as a tincture, ointment, and powder, taken orally as well as smoked. King James I was very much opposed to its use. His *'Counterblaste to Tobacco'* was published in 1603 as a royal health warning, describing the smoking of tobacco as

'a custom loathsome to the eye, hateful to the nose, harmful to the brain, dangerous to the lungs, and in the black stinking fume thereof, nearest resembling the horrible Stygian smoke of the pit that is bottomless'.

The royal disapproval seems to have been as ineffective in helping hardened smokes to give up as the current government health warnings.

The best Spanish tobacco leaf commanded a high price in England and was exported to Virginia. It was popular because it offered a much milder smoke than the leaf grown by the Virginian Indians. Rolfe and his fellow settlers found this local tobacco very rank and strong. He tried to grow other varieties of the tobacco plant and sent for seed from Trinidad and Orinoco in the Spanish West Indies.

Rolfe found that a variety called Varina seemed to do well in the Henricus soil and Virginia climate. By his second season at Henricus, Rolfe had grown enough 'sweat leaf' of this new milder tobacco to send the first samples to England. It was an immediate commercial success and the London market wanted more. John Rolfe was becoming rich.

Growing tobacco plants in a seed bed on the Chesapeake

'Hearty and best thoughts'

John Rolfe did not just find wealth in Henricus in 1614. The attractive young Indian princess lodging with the Reverend Wittacker caught his eye and a friendship developed. Unaware of this growing attachment, Dale took her with a small army of soldiers including John Rolfe to the Pamunkey River to try to force Powhatan's hand, The English ship was attacked by the local Indians. Dale landed his soldiers and burnt the villages on the shore. He met two of Pocahontas' half-brothers further up the river who were concerned to meet her to make sure that she was well. When they did meet, they were amazed to hear that she had no wish to return to her own people, preferring to stay with the English, and refusing even to discuss the matter!

Rolfe's letter

In Dale's pocket at this meeting was a letter. It had been written by Rolfe and given to another settler to be passed on to Dale at a suitable moment. Rolfe was not at all sure that his letter would get a positive response. Its subject was the very delicate matter of marriage between an Englishman and an American Indian woman. Rolfe set out all the reasons why such a marriage would benefit the Jamestown Colony and assured Dale that mere lust had nothing to do with the matter. It would be *'for the good of the plantation, for the honour of our country, for the glory of God, for his own salvation and for the converting to the true knowledge of God and Jesus Christ an unbelieving creature, namely Pocahontas, to whom my hearty and best thoughts are and have a long time been so entangled and enthralled in so intricate a labyrinth, that I was even a-wearied to unwind myself there-out'*.

John Rolfe's dilemma

'We had captured the American Indian Princess and brought her to our English town. The first minute I layed eyes on her, I fell in love but there was one problem - my people and her people did not get on. Tonight is the night

I'm going to see her and to see if she feels the same way about me. My only fear is that I will go to hell because she is not a English Christian. But it seems that Rebecca fell in love with me as well. I'm glad that she loves me. I'm going to send a letter to Powhatan for permission to marry his daughter Pocahontas'. *(by Jade S.)*

Alexander Whittaker must have smiled when he heard that Rolfe wanted to marry Pocahontas for the '*sake of her religious conversion*'. He already knew that she wanted to become a Christian. Governor Dale immediately saw the advantages of such a match in terms of the relationship between the English and her people and especially her father. He gave his approval for the wedding. Pocahontas was brought to Jamestown. She was baptised and given a new Christian name, Rebecca. In the Bible story of the marriage of Isaac, the son of Abraham, Rebecca was the woman chosen to be Isaac's wife and given the blessing *'Be the mother of thousands of ten thousands'*.

John Rolfe and Rebecca, better known as Pocahontas, were married on April 5th 1614 in a service from the Church of England Book of Common Prayer. The wedding was probably in the simple wooden church built in 1608 at Jamestown in 1808 before John Smith had left the Colony. The post-holes of that church have recently been discovered by the Jamestown Rediscovery team and the 400th anniversary of the wedding will be celebrated on April 5th 2014. In 1614, Rev Bucke was the Minister at Jamestown and would have married the couple. After the wedding, Rolfe and Pocahontas probably moved back to live on Rolfe's farm not far from Henricus. A son, Thomas, was born in the following year.

The Rolfe-Pocahontas marriage brought peace between the English and Powhatan's people. The great chief sent a message to Governor Dale. Too many of his men and of the English had been killed. He was now very old and wished to end his days in peace. Powhatan decided to move away from the English, leaving them free to occupy his territories because '*my country is large enough*'.

Certificate of Marriage Between

Mr John Rolfe, widower,
born 6 May 1585, Heacham, Norfolk, England:

and

The Princess Pocahontas alias Rebecca
born 17 September 1595, Gloucester side on York River, Virginia:

Witnessed
by Governor Thomas Dale, Opachisco (Uncle of the Bride), and two of his sons.
5th April 1614

(by Jack)

Becoming Tassentasses

A neighbouring tribe, the Chickahominy, even decided to become subjects of King James and changed their name to '*tassantasses*', their word for Englishmen. John Rolfe and many of the others at Henricus began to grow their new tobacco variety in commercial quantities and to export it to England. He sent four barrels of leaf in 1614. Two years later, 2,300 pounds were sent by all the farmers and over 18,000 pounds in the following year. Virginia at last had a cash crop which could sustain the Colony.

The peace of Pocahontas

The great marriage between John Rolfe and Pocahontas created an eight-year peace between the English and the Powhatans; this was known as the 'Peace of Pocahontas' saving hundreds of lives. Some people in Virginia today believe they are direct descendants of Pocahontas through their son Thomas, so she did become 'the mother of thousands'.

(by Jack)

Virginia lottery

In London, the Virginia Company was still trying to persuade people to go to Virginia. So many at Jamestown had died that the colony could only be developed by sending fresh recruits. Even the climate was bad for much of the year. Newcomers were lucky to survive their first sweltering summer. Those who did were said to be '*seasoned*', hardened off to last a few more months. The Company also needed to raise money to invest in the Colony. They had tried selling shares, but the investors had got tired of losing their money. Virginia just did not make a profit. There was no gold and no way through to the Pacific Ocean.

The company had tried government by elected President and by Council but the only leader who had been able to hold things together during the first two years, John Smith, had gone home. They had tried to find a man strong enough to appoint as overall Governor, but he too fell sick and came home. They had declared martial law which was so harsh that the English, even though they were used to a punitive Common Law, found it barbaric. In spite of the support of the Church and the hope that American Indians would become Christians, the share holders had seen no return on their money.

The Virginia Company cut the cost of supplying the new colony by getting the King to agree that all exports to Virginia would be duty free. Those whom they described as '*wicked imps……who to cover their own lewdness do fill men's ears with false reports of their miserable and perilous life in Virginia*' were to be silenced by prosecution, both in Virginia and England. Finally, the Company hit on a new idea and applied for permission to set up a lottery. If the hope of gold in America proved false, perhaps more immediate rewards of gold in London would do the trick.

The first prize of this annual lottery was to be £1000, a huge sum of money in 1612. Again, the churches backed the venture and some even bought tickets. One church won the £500 second prize. The lottery was an immediate success, raising more money than the last share issue, with none of the long-term costs of promising to pay dividends on the shares. But by the second and third round, interest was dropping again. When the news of the conversion of Pocahontas and her marriage to John Rolfe reached London, the Company saw a great opportunity to boost interest in their Colony and in their lottery. If Londoners could see Pocahontas for themselves as the evidence of the success of both evangelism and good relations with the Indians, the lottery tickets would fly out of the hands of the sellers. So they planned to bring her to London, the attractive, intelligent young woman who had decided to wed John Rolfe.

Sir Thomas Dale had completed his five year term of service with the Company and was returning home. Arrangements were made for the Rolfes and their baby son to sail from Jamestown to London with Dale. Pocahontas was accompanied by a team of Powhatan young women. Her father, Powhatan, sent one of his priests or shamans, Uttamatomakkin, to find out about the English. He had instructions to carry a stick wherever he went and to make a mark on the stick with his knife for every Englishman that he saw. They sailed in Argall's ship with a cargo of Rolfe's tobacco in the hold. It was the same vessel and Captain that had kidnapped Pocahontas and taken her to Jamestown, but Pocahontas seems not to have raised any objection.

6. Going to England

It was the first time that any of the Powhatans on the ship had crossed the Atlantic Ocean, although there had been other Algonquian-speaking Indians taken by force across to Europe. When the ship reached Plymouth in June 1616, the Rolfe family went ashore and were taken by coach to London, a rough and bumpy trip of about a week, staying at coaching inns along the road. Excited crowds milled around the first American Indian Princess seen in England. Uttamatomakkin soon gave up cutting notches on his stick. In London, the Virginia Company had arranged for the Rolfes to stay at an inn on Ludgate Hill near to the old St Paul's Cathedral. It was called the *'Belle Sauvage'*, and was not the most comfortable of lodgings, but the cost was within the Company's budget. Was the name a coincidence, or perhaps it was renamed after Pocahontas's arrival?

Just after the Rolfes reached England, Captain John Smith, who was living in London, published his new book. It was an account of New England, the product of his 1614 voyage to explore the coast of the northern part of what was still called Virginia. He had sailed an open shallop from near to the French colony at Mont Desert Island in the far north to Cape Cod, mapping the whole coastline. On his return to England, Smith had published a map of what he called 'New England'.

When Smith learnt that the Virginia Company proposed to bring Pocahontas to London, he decided to write a letter of introduction on her behalf to Queen Anne. This letter contained the first account of the incident in Powhatan's long-house nine years before, when he claimed that his life had been saved by the great Chief's daughter. Smith described the debt he owed to this Indian Princess and asked the Queen to receive her as a royal visitor. He must have been aware of the Company's plans to use her as a curiosity to help promote the Virginia lottery at minimum cost, cheap lodgings in the city and the paltry sum of £4 a week to pay for all her expenses.

Smith's letter did the trick. Although the Queen never replied, Pocahontas was soon introduced to London society by Lord and Lady Delaware, the former Governor of Virginia and his wife. She was entertained by the Bishop of London, invited to plays and balls and treated with great respect and courtesy. Throughout all this attention, she conducted herself with all the grace and dignity of a Princess. Smith had called her the '*non-pareil*' of her people, an attractive and intelligent young woman, able to adapt to a strange land and trained at Henricus and Jamestown in the niceties of English etiquette.

While Pocahontas was being entertained by London society, Uttamatomakkin, Powhatan's shaman, was invited to discuss Indian religion with a London vicar, the Rev

Samuel Purchas. He was a friend of John Smith and was collecting accounts of life in early Virginia for his book *'Purchas His Pilgrimage or Relations of the World and the Religions observed in all ages and Places discovered from the Creation unto this present'*. It was a project as ambitious as its title was long and Purchas was keen to include an account of Indian religious practice from the most authoritative source, Powhatan's shaman.

Meeting the King and Queen

In all this social whirl around Pocahontas, John Rolfe seems to have been a spectator.

Queen Anne, wife of King James I of England and Scotland

Presented formally to the Queen, Pocahontas was impressed by her regal presence. However, when she was required to kneel before the King, she could not believe that the stout, unwashed and scruffy man before her was the great King James in person.

Letter to America

Lord Powhatan,
Supreme Chief of all the Powhatan,
Brave Warrior, Wise Leader

We write to advise you that we have arrived in England safely. Your brave and beautiful daughter, Pocahontas, received a wonderful welcome from the people of London, which honoured you greatly, noble chief. They thought her given name quite unusual and charming, but of course we now use her Christian name, the lady Rebecca. She is still not used to the business here compared to Virginia.

We were invited to meet my Queen on Sunday; however, I have to advise you that the princess grows weaker each day, becoming very ill. I don't really know if she'll survive. If her health worsens then I will bring her back to you immediately so you can care for her.

Yours sincerely,
John Rolfe.

(by Alisha and Megan)

Pocahontas enjoyed her life in London. While she was there, she sat for a portrait by a young Dutch engraver, Simon van de Passe. He had already completed an engraved portrait of Captain John Smith, with the confident bearded face of an experienced soldier. Pocahontas' picture is of a gaunt woman who seems to be much older than her twenty years. She is dressed as a seventeenth century English woman of quality, complete with Prince of Wales feathers in her hand and a high hat.

Copy of the Van der Passe portrait of Pocahontas in the stained glass window in Willoughby Church

    These are the only images from life of either character which have survived to our day although there are many other pictures which claim to be of Pocahontas.

Did Pocahontas visit Heacham?

With Mr and Mrs John Rolfe now in England, it might be thought natural for them to call in to meet John's family in Heacham. That is what a twenty-first Century couple would do and there is a strong tradition in Heacham that the visit did take place at some time in their relatively short visit to England. But there is no record of such a visit. Pocahontas was accompanied to England by a retinue of her fathers' people, led by her sister Matachana and her brother-in-law Uttamatakin, one of Powhatan's shamans. If she had travelled with her young son to meet John's relatives at Heacham, surely she would have taken her family and advisers with her. Such an exotic party of American Indians would have been noted by someone, especially in rural Norfolk, but there is not trace.

There is another local tradition in Heacham, that not only did she visit Heacham Hall in 1616, but she planted a mulberry tree there. James I had encouraged the planting of such trees to support an English silk industry as silk-worm fed on mulberry. There are ancient mulberrries still growing all over England from that period. The one at Christ's College, Cambridge, was planted by the poet John Milton, and there is an even older tree at Syon House, planted by the Earl of Northumberland. Pocahontas may well have seen this tree as she is known to have stayed at Brentford nearby. The Earl was the older brother of Governor Henry Percy of Jamestown and it is likely that he met Pocahontas at Syon House.

There is an old mulberry at Heacham, still growing in the farm that was once part of the Manor. There is even a 'petrified tree trunk' said to be a mulberry stored in the village and said to be 'Pocahontas' mulberry', but, sadly, in neither of these cases can the 'local tradition' of Pocahontas' mulberry tree be verified.

St Mary's Church does hold one link with the faith of that period in the form of fine copy of the King James Bible, with 1617 printed on the frontispiece.

For nearly four hundred years, this bible, believed to have been once owned by the Rolfe family, has been kept in St Mary's Church. Some in Heacham think that this could be the Bible which the King and Queen Anne are said to have given to Pocahontas at the Twelfth Night Masque they all attended in London. But there is no way of confirming that 'local legend' as two of the front pages are missing and no record in Court papers has yet been found.

Pocahontas falls ill

Seventeenth century London was a dangerous place. The plague, tuberculosis, pneumonia and all the diseases we now protect children against, were frequent visitors to the narrow streets and dark alleys of the overcrowded capital. They took their toll of young and old alike. Damp houses, smoking chimneys and filthy streets sapped the resistance even of the strong. Those who came from warmer climates with no natural immunity to our diseases were especially vulnerable.

Pocahontas in England by Megan

Pocahontas was already ill when her portrait was engraved. She was moved with her child out of the city to the cleaner air of Brentford, then a village to the west of

London. It was to Brentford that John Smith eventually went to visit her.

Pocahontas had been a child of ten or eleven when she had known him in Jamestown. She was the cart-wheeling girl playing with the boys of the English settlement and he the tough, capable soldier of twenty seven. She had been in London for the best part of a year before he made any direct attempt to see her. Although she had been told in Virginia that he was dead, here he was, living in London.

She must call him 'father'

When he first walked back into her life after all those years, her reaction was one of shock. She could not speak, although Smith knew that she was fluent in English. Rolfe suggested that they leave her for a time to compose herself.

When they returned, and when Smith tried to explain, she interrupted him. Had he not called Powhatan 'father', when he had come as a stranger to their land, and now she must call him 'father'. Smith tried to dissuade her. He could not permit her, a Princess, to call him 'father' when in London. He was a mere Captain and English society would not understand what she meant by this deference to him.

If at first Pocahontas had been shocked, she was then angry with Captain John Smith. How could he be afraid? Had he shown fear when he came into her country and to her father? Rather it was Powhatan who had been afraid and all his people of what this coming might mean. She would always be his 'child' and she would think of him as her 'father' and always her countryman. Her real father had warned her that the English were liars and now she knew that it was true. The Englishman was not dead, but he had ignored her for far too long.

Pocahontas angry with Captain John Smith by Katherine C.

In his embarrassment, Smith took his leave of Pocahontas and never saw her again. She was now the wife of an Englishman and the mother of his child. She must put behind her the childhood friendship which could so easily be misunderstood.

But even as her health got worse, John Rolfe was impatient to get back to his tobacco farm. The Company had appointed him Secretary of the Virginia Colony and he had official duties to perform. Captain Argall would soon be sailing from London and it was agreed that the Rolfes would go back to Virginia with him. For a time the winter delayed their sailing, but when the weather improved, John Rolfe insisted that they join Argall's ship, the *George*, and set off down the Thames estuary. He seemed not to know how ill his wife had become.

Death at Gravesend

But Pocahontas never saw her father in Tsenacomoco again. The ship sailed down the River Thames and, off the Kent port of Gravesend, Pocahontas knew that she was dying. She pleaded with Rolfe to be taken ashore. She was carried onto the wharf and they must have found lodgings at a riverside inn. With her husband beside her bed, perhaps holding the two-year-old Thomas in his lap, it was Pocahontas who spoke words of comfort. '*All must die,*' she said, '*'tis enough that the child liveth.*'

> **Pocahontas is dead – news from Gravesend**
>
> *The beautiful Pocahontas has just passed away in Gravesend on the coast of Kent with her beloved husband John Rolfe at the side of her bed. Her sad father Powhatan didn't even get to say goodbye to his beautiful daughter. John Rolfe is so upset since his last wife died of a disease just like this so he has now lost two wives. Her little boy Thomas was on the ship with her at the time so at least he was able to say goodbye to his mum.*
>
> *(by Alisha)*

They buried her in the chancel of St George's Church, as the register records, although it must have been done in a hurry as the Christian name of the husband is wrong, and her name is given as Wroffe, not Rolfe. The chancel tomb within the church was used for the burials of Vicars of the Parish and important local gentry, a fitting place for a Princess who died so far from her own people.

The burial was recorded in the register of St George's Parish Church, Gravesend:

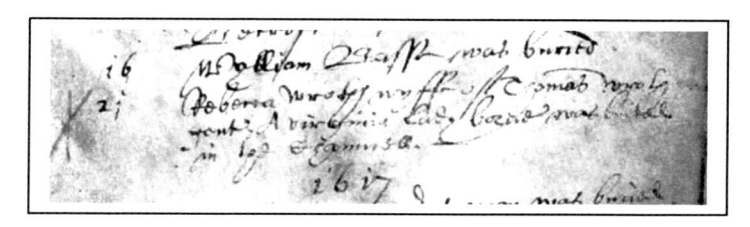

'1617 March 21 Rebecca Wrothe wyffe of Thomas Wroth gent. A Virginia Lady was buried in the Chauncell.'

When St George's Church caught fire and burnt down in 1732, the exact place of her burial was lost. The old chancel graves were removed and the remains reburied in a common grave so that the bones of this brave young woman were mixed with all the others buried there and so have been lost. In spite of many attempts to find them in the Gravesend earth, they can rever be returned to her people in Virginia. Nevertheless, this is the place to which many Americans come to pay their respects to the woman whose marriage brought together two peoples, the English and the subjects of Powhatan, her father.

John Rolfe and their child, Thomas, left her there in Gravesend and went back on board the *George*. Captain Argall sailed on out into the North Sea and round into the Channel. Thomas was also ill and by the time they reached Plymouth, Argall persuaded Rolfe that the child would not survive the long Atlantic crossing. So Thomas was taken ashore and left in the care of a stranger as guardian while his father sent an urgent letter to his brother who was a rich merchant in London. Henry Rolfe came down to Devon and accepted responsibility for his nephew's care and upbringing.

Leaving his motherless son behind, John Rolfe rejoined the *George* and sailed back to Jamestown to take up his duties as Secretary and, more importantly, to get on with the serious and highly profitable business of growing more and more tobacco.

The Colony prospers

Although Pocahontas was no longer there to embody the peace between Powhatan and the English, her influence lived on and peace continued. Powhatan was now an old man. He handed over his responsibility as Werowance to his brothers before he died in April 1618, one year after his daughter. Captain Argall became the Deputy Governor of the Colony for a time, before a new regime took over in the person of Sir George Yeardley, a kindly governor in comparison with Sir Thomas Dale. Tobacco farming became so popular that growing food was of little interest and little profit.

Yeardley decided to distribute land to the settlers and many received large estates. They were encouraged to 'build houses and clear ground ready to plant' which they did with enthusiasm, establishing tobacco plantations some of which exist to this day. With the new property rights came a new form of government, the General Assembly of Burgesses. Those who were men and owned land could elect their own representatives.It was the beginnings of democracy in America. The Burgesses first met in the church at Jamestown in July 1619, in sweltering heat, with the Rev Richard Bucke as Chaplain. Among the issues that they considered were the the keeping of the peace, dealing with drunkenness and encouraging land holders to plant food crops as well as tobacco. They also agreed that the English settlers' conduct towards the Indians should always be fair, although subsequently the English drove most of the Virginian Indians out of their traditional hunting lands.

Death on the James

New settlements spread out along both banks of the James River. The English gave little thought how they might defend the scattered tobacco farms from attack. The Indians were even encouraged to live amongst the English, working on the plantations and being paid in tobacco which became the currency of the Colony. On the surface at least, prosperity and peaceful co-existence seemed to be well established. But Powhatan's younger brother, Openchancanough, had decided that the English must be driven out before they occupied all of his lands.

The massacre of the English on March 22nd 1622

March 22nd 1622 started like any other day on the tobacco plantations. Englishmen and Indians went to work in the fields. Indians brought venison and furs to the farmhouses to trade with the women. But the Indians had planned slaughter. Using the settlers' own tools and weapons, the Powhatans turned on the English, killing men, women and children. By nightfall, 347 out of the 1400 English in settlements along the river were known to be dead. The survivors were scattered in small groups into the woods or still in relative safety in Jamestown.

Five years after Pocahontas had been laid to rest in Gravesend, the peace between her people and the English ended. News of the massacre did not reach England until July of that year and the indignant reaction was predictable. The Indians had now proved their viciousness and must be made to pay for their treachery. King James sent a large cargo of weapons and armour out to reinforce the colony from the stock of obsolete equipment held in the Tower of London, and the long process of ridding the colony of the Indian menace began. Powhatan's brother's decision to attack the English would, in the end, bring about the death of many of his own people.

Doubts about John Rolfe's death

What really happened to John Rolfe? Was he in fact killed with the others in a morning of blood? He had married for a third time shortly after returning to Virginia and lived in comfort on his farm named Varina. Respected as their Secretary and leading businessman, Rolfe prospered until March 1621 when he wrote a will, witnessed by Rev Richard Bucke. He must have fallen ill. This suggests that he was spared the massacre, dying just before March 22nd 1622 but there is no grave to mark Rolfe's passing.

His son, Thomas, the child he had with Pocahontas, was brought up in England by his uncle, Henry, who was a rich merchant in London and a member of the Virginia Company. Thomas returned to Virginia as a young man in his twenties well after the massacre, and became Captain of Fort James. He married an English girl whose father owned more land near Henrico. Thomas also inherited land from both his Indian grandfather and English father and became a wealthy farmer in his own right. There is a grave slab in a garden in the city of Hopewell on the James River which some claim marks the place of Thomas' burial. It lies on land that was once owned by Colonel Bowling, of the family into which Thomas' only daughter married. She had a son and five daughters. From these, countless Virginian families claim to have the blood of Pocahontas in their veins.

7. Pocahontas' people

Four hundred years after the English first came to Jamestown, are there any of Pocahontas' people left in the State of Virginia? In the 17th C, as the English pushed the Powhatans out of their hunting lands, there were two small areas which were designated as Indian reservations. They been occupied by the Pamunkey and Mattaponi peoples ever since.

Although there is now very little land owned by Indian communities, there are centres clustered around churches, such as the Pamunkey Baptist Church. There are also community centres maintained by the Chickahominy, the Rappahannock, the Nansemond, the Nottaway and the Monacan peoples in the areas which they once occupied. Perhaps it is not surprising that these communities have linked up with the Baptists and other Non-Conformist churches rather than the Anglican/Episcopalian Church of the original Jamestown settlers. The State of Virginia has recognised eight of the original tribes but they are still trying to get Federal recognition.

The Pamunkey Baptist Church

When the 400th Anniversary of the Founding of Jamestown was being planned for 2007, for the Indian community this was was more of a commemoration than a celebration, given the sad history of their people since the coming of the English to Jamestown. To acknowledge this, UK Committee for Jamestown 2007 invited the Virginian Indian tribes to send a representative group of their leaders and their families back to England in 2006, to visit Gravesend and other historic sites, including a reception at the Elizabethan Cobham Hall in Kent.

There, the representative of Her Majesty the Queen, the Lord Lieutenant of the County of Kent, received from Chief Anne Richardson of the Rappahannock Tribe a wedding band of Virginian gold. It symbolised the bringing together of two people in the marriage of Pocahontas to John Rolfe. The group then danced in the grounds of Cobham Hall to mark the occasion.

When President George W Bush came to Jamestown to commemorate Jamestown 2007, the Chief of the Chickahominy people, Chief Stephen R Adkins was invited to address the people of the United States of America as a representative of the seven Indian Tribes of the Commonwealth of Virginia:

'Life has not been easy for Virginia's indigenous peoples, but to the person we are proud to be Virginians and Americans. Most tribal members across the Commonwealth are proud to be a part of a commemoration that has provided an opportunity for us to tell our story and to let the world know that descendants of some of the sovereign nations who greeted the settlers on the shores of the Powhatan River (James River) at Tsenacomoco are still here.'

Chief Stephen Adkins at Jamestown 2007

8. And is it true?

Matoake   Grandfather, tell me the story of the white men who stole our princess Pocahontas Snow Feather..

Grandfather   It all started a long time ago …it was the time of the bear, when the land was invaded by savage whiteskins.

Matoake   What happened to our ancient ones?

Grandfather   They were viciously cut down by the deadly firesticks that the whiteskins brought on their tall seaships.

Matoake   Tell me about the young maiden and how she saved the English sea captain.

Grandfather   Our brave warriors captured the chief of the whiteskins. Wise Powhatten sentenced the savage to death. Little snow feather came to his rescue; she jumped between the clubs and the whiteskin and begged her father to spare his life.

Matoake   But why? When he was a savage?

Grandfather   Because her heart was filled with mercy.

Matoake   And did the white men thank our people for their kindness?

Grandfather   No, they attacked us with firesticks and killed many of our people.

Matoake   Why did our beautiful Snow Feather take food to the savages?

Grandfather   Young Matoake, if little Snow Feather hadn't fed the savages, they would have died.

Matoake   And was there peace between the savages and our people?

Grandfather   For a little while, but noble Powhatan wanted firesticks to take revenge on the whiteskins and become the most powerful chief of the Algonquian peoples.

Matoake   Is it true that Matoake Snow Feather was taken prisoner by the English?

Grandfather   Pocahontas Snow Feather was tempted by the English to go on board one of their seaships. But once on board, they refused to let her go.

Matoake   And did she escape the whiteskins?

Grandfather   No, they made her Christian and she was baptised Rebecca.

Matoake   Rebecca? That's a funny name! And is it true that she married a whiteskin?

Grandfather   Yes, to bring peace between our peoples, she married whiteskin Rolfe, a pipe smoker of the new plant the whiteskins call tobacco.

Matoake   And is it true that Naughty Little One crossed the Great Sea to the land of the whiteskins?

Grandfather   It is said that Pocahontas lived only a few moons more before she passed into the realm of the Spirits.

**All   Remember brave Matoake Snow Feather.
May her name live long in our histories.**

(by the Year 6 pupils of Heacham Junior School, Norfolk, England)

Postscript

If you want to know more about what happened to those who made the settlement of Jamestown possible, read the other books in this American Roots in English Soil (ARIES) series: *'Captain John Smith and the Founding of America', 'Captain Christopher Newport of Limehouse and Virgnia' and 'Bartholomew Gosnold of Otley and America'.*

Thirteen years after Jamestown was first established, the Pilgrim Fathers landed at Plymouth near Cape Cod and established their settlement. Ten years after that, the Massachusetts Bay Company settled the area to the north of Plymouth and founded the large colony which grew into the City of Boston, Massachusetts. Not long after Plymouth, the Catholics established their first settlements in Maryland. All these developments in early American history have their roots in the rich soil of Eastern England.

Some feature in other titles in the American Roots in English Soil (ARIES) series: *'Robert Troublechurch Browne of Tolethorpe and the Separatists', 'William Brewster of the Pilgrim Fathers' and 'Admiral of New England – Captain John Smith and the American Dream'..*

But we should never forget that the first permanent English-speaking settlement was established at Jamestown, Virginia, in May 1607.

Sources

We used the following sources to research this book

Arber, Edward Ed. *'Captain John Smith Complete Works'* Birmingham. 1884

Barbour, Philip *'Pocahontas and her World'* Robert Hale 1969 and *'The Three Worlds of Captain John Smith'*. Houghton Miflin. 1964

Doherty, Kieron *'To Conquer is to live'* Twenty-first Century 2001 *

Gittings, J G *'Pocahontas an American Indian Princess*, Hulton Educational 1971*

Grant, Sally *'Pocahontas Indian Princess alias Mrs Rolfe'* The Larks Press 1995

Horn, James *'A Land as God Made it – Jamestown and the birth of America'* Basic Books 2005

Hume, Ivor Noel *'The Virginia Adventure'*. Knopf. 1994

Kelso, William M and Beverley Straube *'Jamestown Rediscovery 1994-2004'* APVA 2004

Kelso, William M *'Jamestown the Buried Truth'* University of Virginia Press 2006

Morey, Dennis A J *'Sir Thomas Dale – unrecognised father of the Nation'* The Henricus Foundation

Mossiker, Frances *'Pocahontas – the life and legend'* Da Capo Press edition 1996

Price, David A *'Love and Hate in Jamestown'* Knopf. 2003

Rountree, Helen *'Pocahontas, Powhatan and Opechancanough – three lives changed by Jamestown'* Univ. of Virginia Press 2005

Shakespeare, William *The Complete Works* Ed. Peter Alexander. Collins. 1951

Wright Hale, Edward *'Jamestown Narratives'*. Roundhouse. 1998

  * books written for young people

and the following websites:
Jamestown-Yorktown Foundation at www.jamestown2007.org/ and at www.historyisfun.org/jamestown/jamestown.cfm

'Historic Jamestowne' at www.historicjamestowne.org/index/php

Association for the Preservation of Virginian Antiquities at www.apva.org.

Virtual Jamestown Project at www.virtualjamestown.org/

Thanks

Many individuals have helped us with this book and we would like to thank them all.

In Heacham, Norfolk, UK:

Mrs Nicky Darley, Headteacher, Mr Brian Griffin and Mrs Carolyn Ward, Y6 Teachers, and the Staff and Governors of Heacham Junior School

Mr Henry Head and the Staff of Norfolk Lavender,

Mr John Wallis, Mr Maurice Gibbons, Mr Jim Agate, Mrs Mary Pishorn, Mrs Stella Gooch

Mrs Christine Dean of St Mary's Church, Heacham

In Lincolnshire, UK

Mrs Molly Burkett of Barny Books, Mr Geof Allinson of Allinson Print, Mr John Loft of Julian Bower, Mr Hugo Spiegl of Spiegl Print

In Virginia, USA

Dr and Mrs Bill Kelso of Jamestown and Mr and Mrs Richard Hanks Nicholl of Williamsburg.

and many others who have helped with layout advice, historical information and patience when our interest in American history got in the way of other priorities.